THE SHADE-SELLER
New and Selected Poems

Also by the Author

Poetry
LET EACH MAN REMEMBER
FOR THE UNLOST
THE HUMAN CLIMATE
THE ANIMAL INSIDE

Prose
With Wm. R. Mueller
GENET AND IONESCO:
PLAYWRIGHTS OF SILENCE
THE TESTAMENT OF SAMUEL BECKETT

Josephine Jacobsen

THE
SHADE-SELLER

New and Selected Poems

Doubleday & Company, Inc.   Garden City, New York   1974

ISBN: 0-385-00996-8 Trade
0-385-00997-6 Paperbound
Library of Congress Catalog Card Number 73–10860
Copyright © 1946, 1953, 1969, 1974 by Josephine Jacobsen
All Rights Reserved
Printed in the United States of America
First Edition

Acknowledgment is made to the following for permission to reprint material which they have published previously: all of the poems selected from *Let Each Man Remember* were previously published in that volume by The Kaleidograph Press, Dallas, Texas, Copyright © 1940.

Each of the poems selected from *The Animal Inside* was previously published in that volume by The Ohio University Press, copyright © 1967 and is reprinted by permission.

The Shade-Seller, The Interrupted, Bush Christmas Eve first appeared in *Commonweal,* Copyright © 1965, 1969, 1973 Commonweal Publishing Co., Inc.; *The Crabracers, The Emperor's Cook, Notes from a Lenten Bar* in *Poetry Newsletter,* Copyright © 1972 Temple University; *Anemones at Lindos/The Parthenon Frieze, The Foreign Lands,* © 1968, 1970, 1973 by The New York Times Company. Reprinted by permission; *The Chanterelles, Vantage,* copyright © 1970 by Gilman School; *Night Patrol, The Mexican Peacock, The Lovers* in *The New Yorker,* © 1968, 1972, 1973 by the New Yorker Magazine, Inc.; *Return from Delphi, In the Crevice of Time, Arrival, Destinations, Ghosts at Khe Sanh, The Planet* in *Poetry,* copyright © 1966, 1968, 1970 by Modern Poetry Association; *Future Green, Dishwasher as Absolution* in *New Letters,* copyright © 1972 the Curators of the University of Missouri; *A Reason of Numbers,* in *Sunstone Review,* copyright © 1972 by Sunstone Review and Press, Inc.; *The Wild, Birdsong of the Lesser Poet, Kamadhenu,* copyright © 1972 by G. S. Chandra; *The Class,* reprinted by permission of The New Republic, © 1970 Harrison-Blaine of New Jersey, Inc.

For ERIC

CONTENTS

NEW POEMS

From LET EACH MAN REMEMBER

From FOR THE UNLOST

From THE HUMAN CLIMATE

From THE ANIMAL INSIDE

NEW POEMS

THE SHADE-SELLER

FOR A. R. AMMONS

"Sombra?"
he asked us from his little booth. And shade
we bought to leave our car in.

By noon
the sand was a mealy fire; we crossed by planks
to the Revolcadero sea.

One day
we were later and hotter; and he peered out
and "No hay sombra!" he told us.

That day
when we came back to our metal box, frightened
we breathed for a terrible instant

the air
fiery and loud of the hooked fish.
Quick! Quick! Our silver key!

Sometimes
now I dream of the shade-seller; from his dark
he leans, and "sombra . . ." I tell him.

There is
candescent sand and a great noise of heat
and it is I who speak that word

heavy
and wide and green. O may he never
answer my one with three.

AN ABSENCE OF SLAVES

The Greek guide
said:
"I want you to remember one thing."
With her deep voice and curly
hair
and small shocked shoes, she said,
"This is our pride:

this was free
labor:
free men built this Par-
thenon. Athenians
left fold and press and field
and harbor:
gave no slavery."

The sun broke
on glorious stone, ripped from the dark
quarry; she said: "The city
sent a slave
to each man's yoke,
oil press and furrow,
to free for toil the free Greek:

the free raised these!" she cried
to the blue sky and honey-
veined columns. "This is
no pyramid." And I saw
the loins and wrists
and bones and tendons of those disprized
who in absence reared the great frieze.

THE WILD PARROTS OF BLOODY BAY

Up from Bloody Bay are the hills
where the wild parrots live.
In pairs they fly
high and dark with harsh faint cries.

In the last sunlight the hurricane-
stripped trees point up up
to where in that thin soft gold air
they wheel and fly fast and together away.

But they descend too: on a distant bare tree
like Chinese ornaments,
without motion or pity
they sit burning in their own green:

then soundless up and off, careening
over the crests. To mock and to redeem
the obscene cracker and the puppet syllable
come the faint wild harsh screams.

THE ISLANDS

On a bad night
    the brain cells stored with the honey of happiness
live on themselves:

palms fall upward, strong like noisy
    fountains:
air-plants breathe, silent in
    leafy reaches up a greenness:

and stilted crabs like most devious ghosts
    raise themselves, running sidewise
down gold sands to the winking tide.
    The islands lean and love us in the dark.

But then the boa-constrictor rustles tin
    under the ruined house: and the bats glimmer
hunting the angles of the dusk:
    your face disappears into dead vines
and the real dread
    invests itself in forms I did not fear.

Go altogether, islands. Go, and wait,
    waiting in your true distance
and most lovely fact.

THE CRABRACERS

Suddenly, the music is mute; all the keys
lock up their notes that divided the sinuous palmfronds.
Sixty chairs go back with a mingled metal sound;
and drinks in hand all are off to the races.

The crabs are under a bowl with a giant bulb—
very hot, very bright—and are not apt to balk.
The bowl is the center of a generous circle in chalk,
and a circle of faces is a wheel with the crabs as its hub.

Then the bowl goes up, and the bets; and the crabs go.
On the strange concrete, springy under the cheers,
hard-shelled, bow-legged, in a wandering veer.
The motionless, dart sidewise; the most rapid, slows

a sinful inch from the chalk. Screams, and new highs.
A lumbering lurker puts a pincer over.
A hundred yards away the salt sea says, I cover
the sand, the sand says, I return my prizes.

The Caribbean is near to the crabs, and the sand is closer,
pitted with holes in its heaved dryness; thick
with viscous moonlight where the edges are slick.
The crabs are back in the bowl, and the bulb is hotter.

Money has changed hands. The reassured people,
closer, brighter, are ready for the second race.
The tide times the people, as the bowl is raised,
hub of a circle beyond the crabs' circle.

ANEMONES AT LINDOS

At high Lindos the sanctuary
fire burns by no altar
but in the seawind it moves
on the ground running
over the stones.

THE SPARROWS AT DELPHI

Sparrows
are in the Treasury of Athens, in the holes
between the pale honey-veined blocks;
the sparrows are whole
and have not been
restored.
Not even a beak or a wing-tip is
chipped.
To the hollow spaces of the empty Athe-
nian Treasury
on the god's slope at Delphi
go in the sparrows.

THE PARTHENON FRIEZE

On the Thessalian plain
almond and apricot still
in this sun stir from,
the grasses lift after,
the galloping of the invisible horses,
the wind of their passage
the great thighs' rush
the kindling manes
the hooves that sprang

to stone.

THE FOREIGN LANDS

I saw a mongoose this morning ripple down the scarp,
hot blood over cold dew, about his savage trades;
up up over the crater lake, from where they screamed and flew
in pairs, the wild parrots drop down out of the upper air
to settle on blasted boughs and wait out dark.

Lizards live in my tree; puff out their throats
in a passion of silence, grow bold second tails under
                                                    my very eyes;
insect-still, against the sky wait in a profile so old
it stirs my hair. Last night, by the steps, at my bare
foot, made out of tough cool dusk a toad was crouched.

Born travelers must and will have terra incognita:
wharf, port, the treecrest trace, fog's rumor of a coast.
But that escaping ghost, the genius of the place,
strangeness, moves its kin outward as the keel comes in.
Poor traveler, helplessly at home in Zanzibar, in
                                            Tierra del Fuego.

Timid or brazen, humble, acquisitive
traveler, this territory will not pall:
toad, parrot, the alien small, feathered, webbed, furry;
lizard, mongoose and bat, they loom like lands,
swing like stars, I watch; and wish to, may not, inherit.

9

THE CHANTERELLES

Near the eighth tee, sixty yards off into the woods from the
green links,
out of the dark spongy soil, yellow as finches or butter
the chanterelles grew suddenly by the black wet trunks
of firs in the sopping glade, where it was always later.

We were going home to cook our feast in cream and Neufchâtel
and onions, to devour it together close to the first flames
smelling of resin. Other mushrooms grew with the chanterelles,
some single, breastbone white; others the color of dust,
the color of rain.

A furious chipmunk dug where something was buried
and prized; a big bird, pumping, blundered over us, once.
Food and fire and love waited. At the end, we hurried
our damp fingers. We had enough, perhaps in every sense.

In the needles' thick silence the air smelled of thunder,
our hands were cold on the fluty underpart;
when we straightened our backs, the pale mushrooms
were paler.
As we came out on the links nothing moved behind us
except the dark.

The chanterelles were royal; food and summers we ate;
yet, in their equinoxial flavor, understood
we dealt as well with cousins-german; with the shapes
of different mushrooms, near the links, in the mock-up wood.

NIGHT PATROL

The wolf's cousin,
gentled to clown for us,
paces now, forbidden
to be trusted, or trust:
paces the pavement.

The black shoes and the furry toes
pace together on the wide
night street; from the raw light, pace
into the jungle shadows.
The wolf blood courses under hide.
The feet echo; silent go the paws.

A clock strikes winter.
Hunters are cold as hunted.
The dog teaches the man to listen:
something waits in the shadows' center.
The wolf heart knows what is wanted,
called back from a dream unnatural and human.

They walked like mutant friends, in a season's sun;
now they walk like wolves, and know their own.
Their own move toward them: empty, the street
moves toward them, where in this bitter season
cold wolf and wolf meet.

RETURN FROM DELPHI

Coming from Delphi in the rain we met a country funeral.

At Delphi last night traveling the wastes of sky, a bare
round moon went and the stream rushed in the absolute
pause of time, the cold furious sacred stream
away below; the big black mountain
mounted in blackness the milky air.
Oracle in no lair.

"A procession?" Our bus slows in the narrow road,
                                    rain-pricked,
jostling lightly. We look through open windows.

A brilliant morning told us another story:
the water, hill and air being bright; and the god's slope
tumbled with honey-veined milky stone, grew flowers;
his columns stood on stone that allows
yellow blossoms to grow.

"A funeral?" "Yes!" A purple cloth. Then children—boys,
no girls; one holding a cupped flame on a pole, they go;
then the priest's black billows; then on six shoulders
                                    the burden.

Fine as needles the rain began at eleven; in and out
of the holes in the Athenian Treasury the sparrows flew.
Was our magnet columns and blocks? Nonsense! We know,
All of us, what: Apollo.

She is not closed away. She is old.
                    She is lying in cold spring flowers
close to our astonished faces; see how we stare.
On her stonestill breast her rainy hands are crossed;
powerful nose, still lips, she is yellow like stone.

12

One thing brought us to Delphi, the scent of the god;
in the cypress thrust, in the rocks where
we climbed; in our care. In our care.

The feet go past to the earth. The vines like snakes
rear from the earth and petals of almond blow
and alight on the earth. We in our leather seats,
prim animals with the knowledge of death in our eyes,
exchange quick glances of complicity.

The rites, the gifts: it all meant Show
a sign. Speak now.

Beaded with rain in the dusk they are gone.
                              The flame, the tilted
cross, the homage of bearing, the honor of flow-
ers, have turned an old woman toward spring, in the dust
of the olives, in the soil of the vines; the honor was
                              for the passage,
that part of the gesture—the columns broken, unbroken.
For the confrontation of where, of how.

The stone said so.

The quick was the god's gesture—unpredictable,
precious, final. That light on stone, horses that rear
to stone, stone eyes, stone wind, meant one point: the man,
the god, the question. In isolation, the earth's shift,
the light darkening. Old woman, yellow like stone, yours
was no delphic answer. Far and fair
on our dark, silent Athens is there.

HYBRID, HUNTING

That is no wolf
   that bulk insomniac shape
     hungry but furtive:
the simple nightmare and the waking hound
   are child's play:
     but the dark
shape running
   does not belong to noon or night:
a hateful hybrid, wings
   and paws and horns:
     familiar
stranger, fleshed from hopeless odds
   and dubious ends
to make a hunting whole:

the lovely sun
   is traveling
elsewhere, but the hunt
   is here and has a while to run.
Love, love, sleep on, sleep
   here,
     far
as that sun.

THE EMPEROR'S COOK

Laguipière, the Emperor's cook,
gastronomy's artificer and chart,
died in the retreat from Moscow,
having in view to the last the two
great themes of nourishment and art.

Ice-ribbed, the scarecrow dead;
a white vibration meant day.
His feasts froze in his brain.
Once he dreamed of his pupil, Carême;
he thought often of his peer, Bouché.

To the bony end, he thought of high
cuisine, august, enticing.
Finally, the glittering slick world
shone like a wicked cake's
megalomaniac icing.

It was like a bitter, short command,
not of word, or rouble,
but of posthumous honor coveted,
to serve the whole brilliant chef d'oeuvre
for some terrible table.

FUTURE GREEN

Unraped as Amazons, Earth jungles stand.
The dark veins of their rivers
travel a body arcane as a wish.
Only high crests see sun. Everything screams and coughs
and drones till noon falls like a hatchet.
In the steamy stillness your human gaze no more than
                                                    by night
molests the spine of the snake, the alligator's eye.

Lunar tumblers click, wheels whirr, batteries
                                breathe and hum;
on the lunar throughways messages scurry like slaves;
operators yawn from worry;
turn nervously in hunger toward the dark

richness across the brief sky.
Tapping minds resent the lunar day,
turn toward the green wild Earth
abandoned in her intimate recesses

where distance is an inch of green welter;
where what screams from the tree may be a bird or not;
and at furious night, green life that was not worth
                                                its death
refracts from seething trees the urban moon.

A REASON OF NUMBERS

American Express called me last week
to ask who I was.
They had my check, all right, but they
didn't have my number.

They had my name, and my address,
but who was I?
Hurt, I went and looked,
and I was, say, F2035-967-B24.

My checks are perforated with numerals.
Uneasy, I tried signing another name,
hoping the check would bounce. But it was all right:
after three checks signed, respectively, Grendel,

Morgan le Faye and I. M. Croesus
came through perfectly, I realized
that though they hadn't met me they had,
so to speak, my number.

Do you know I got scared?
Suppose someone *else* got my number, I thought,
then who would I be? Well, my address. But people move.
Ridiculous, I have a name.

But people change names when they marry
or steal or go on the stage.
So I thought about a design that does not duplicate itself;
and I looked at a snowflake, magnified.

And, I said, even the sleuths of the Federal
Bureau of Investigation rely on the whorl
of a finger. I began to have dreams
of mutilated hands and snowflakes, melted.

Now I suppose I begin to worry over losing
my inimitable soul.

WINTER'S TALE

Well, why did he do it *then?* I can say,
"Sir, save my little boy ere he die . . ."
That's easy, and has been said a number of times.
You might say all the dust of the earth once said "save . . .";
but the fever failed to go away.

And with the flute-players making all that uproar
no wonder he sent them out
before that ambiguous remark about sleep.
But in that sort of sleep
the little girls who do not get up
       when their hands are taken
are too numerous to mention.

Take brothers: there are many; the limit of that
         relationship
is remote, not to say cloudy.
We know about being set on a brother.
Martha's brother came back to her from the dead;
but there must have been
special circumstances behind it.

Mystery, ah yes. Mystery is of course the essence;
        the root and sap.
How true. And if the first person did answer at the moment
it would be no doubt with something prestigious and
         monosyllabic
like a thunderclap.

19

Yet, when the words come out, over the heads docilely
                                              raised up,
"the maiden," "my brother," "my son," a little stir
goes through the eyes and ears and hands
like wind through the dryest reeds. Private memory, probably,
like a curious retrospective hope.

DISHWASHER AS ABSOLUTION

Red-eyed as Rikki-Tikki glows
her roaring cyclops.
In the fairest sky
the stars come out; still the dark grows.

As bone shined white or shell shined pink,
shriven by motion,
through sudsy tumult
shut in their steamy cell her dishes wink.

On the town dump, she thinks, fire flares;
ants clean a starfish
in the green Antilles;
in Guanajuato vultures ride the airs.

Fish pare the drowned, the fisher cleans his catch;
the slow earth wheels
toward the middle waste:
she leans against the windowsill to watch.

The roar goes into silence, with a click:
the electric sum of absolution
or solution
has appeased the yellow plates' arithmetic.

The red eye shuts; but the stars stand in the bough.
Under the tap
she washes her hands, her hands—
but it is not easy, and nothing tells her, Now!

THE PRIMER

I said in my youth
"they lie to children"
but it is not so.
Mother my goose I know
told me the truth.

I remember that treetop minute.
That was a baby is a woman now;
in a rough wind, it was a broken bough
brought down the cradle with the baby in it.

I had a dumpy friend (you would not know his name,
though he indeed had several), after his fall
lay in live pieces by my garden wall
in a vain tide of epaulets and manes.

I had another friend (and you would know her name),
took up her candle on her way to bed.
She had a steady hand and a yellow head
up the tall stairwell, but the chopper came.

So small they meant to run away, from sightless eyes
three mice ran toward my mind instead;
I seized the shapely knife. They fled
in scarlet haste, the blind and tailless mice.

Cock robin was three birds of a single feather.
Three times cock robin fell when a breeze blew;
eye of fly watched; arrow of sparrow flew:
three times cock robin died in the same weather.

Sheep, cows, meander in the corn and meadow;
soundless the horn, fine, fine my seam;
nothing I feed, but rosy grows my cream.
My blue boy sleeps under the stack's huge shadow.

AT NIGHT

the eye closes:
that retina, three inches for the earth
        and the sky
                shuts its camera eye:
that day
        prepares to die,
be judged—be balanced and even,
        hungry and odd;
be purgatory, be
                débris of heaven.

What small
        metaphors we set
ourselves: the three-inch flinching
                eye, the three-inch tyrant
heart, that took the day and all
adventures in. Or
the heart quailing and the savage
                eye: they can feel
        the wind, the heart hear
sounds: now, small instruments, hush:
        beat softly, heart, shutter yourself,
                eye:
contract and tell your size
        in sleep. Sizes are games. What
                size is just
        to hold
God's windy light,
        the small dry tick of hell?

24

THE WILD

A wild duck, invading the Baltimore zoo's duckpond, was drowned when a tame duck attempted to mate with it. A.P.

The wild is a way of breathing; a kind of breath.
Duck, and wild duck, the adjective
tells; the small sustainer's breath
took her surprised by tameness into that dive.

The wild rides scouring ponies, pillage and rape
to rattle the gates, yes, yes; the sour hut
threatens the pyramid, the ape
sends grass to pierce the noble chariot-rut.

The tame rides disguised, but rides its ponies too.
The tame descends in suffocating feathers,
the tame has tentacles softer than glue,
more masks, even, than hate, more aspects than the weather.

Tame. Wild. Not as a problem you might guess
or calculate—but in a deepest division,
an abyss of hostility, solutionless. Solutionless
because alive: an animosity of vision.

Structured in love to the wild, the wild thing by its nature
can be topped by tameness, by quick tameness beguiled.
But it answers with death. Because the creature
though caught, though owned, though penned, is wild. Wild.

TREATY

Chichicastenango

See us, strangers from the land of embarrassed death,
where it is assumed everyone is always alive
and that the living are more numerous than the dead
who are only a few familiar names: Guatemala!
where everything belongs to the dead. They lend
a lodging in the World under strict laws;
from the tiny huddle the living cautiously closes
the old bargain, paying candles, copal and roses.

Paying roses, incense and candles to the ancestors,
to the owners of the World, a section of which he borrows,
to the watchers and guardians, the Lord of Crevices.
Payment for lodging, World, is 9 wax tapers,
½ pound of incense, 25 pesos of aguardiente,
5 ounces of sugar and 100 cakes of copal:
Hail World, and your owners, Masters of the Knives,
Masters of Rules, here is payment to all dead
Master Masons, Master Builders, Masters of Lead.

The flutes for the house, the flutes all night for dancing,
wandering, chaining, thin and pure, play in the shadow
of that attentive hosting; under their eyes perform
the marimberos and the tamboreros
faint in the hills until the cock calls light;
the corn climbs the barranco at their aegis
and their powerful bird, the purifying vulture
black in the blue, down over the flowers' flame
drops his great shade, silent, in their name.

We can see this. Not even children, playing,
clean children, unobservant and important,
can miss the risky tenure of the house,
can impudently disbelieve the presence:
mountains, barrancos, flutes, marimbas, drums
address the multitude whose eyes we bear.
But now at dusk do not insist on our knowledge.
We are quick shadows, but strangers; who need,
when all is said,
a private love, the English language, and a bed.

THE TERRIBLE NAÏVE

sleepwalk, feed
birdseed to kittens,
dislike arithmetic of
courtesy;

omnipotently shrewd
will whistle
in mirrors; will wrestle,
but only after

securely lashing
your wrists with
their tough
vulnerability;

execute ambushes
with un-
loaded guns, but when
they cry

"I die! I die!"
the dark flood
is your
blood.

BIRDSONG OF THE LESSER POET

Exuding someone's Scotch in a moving mist,
abstracted as he broods upon that grant,
he has an intimate word for those who might assist;
for a bad review, a memory to shame the elephant.

Who would unearth a mine, and fail to work it?
His erstwhile hosts are good for fun and games
that brighten the lumpen-audience on the poetry circuit.
He drops only the most unbreakable names.

Disguised as youth, he can assign all guilt:
his clothes proclaim a sort of permanent stasis.
With a hawk's eye for signs of professional wilt,
he weeds his garden of friends on a monthly basis.

And yet, and yet, to that unattractive head,
and yet, and yet, to that careful, cagey face,
comes now and again the true terrible word;
unearned, the brief visa into some state of grace.

THE MEXICAN PEACOCK

(For Flannery O'Connor)

He presses the eight o'clock dew with short sharp paces,
the tail, laid plume on plume, balanced over the grass
by inches, dipping not touching; the stiff elegant
crest over the head level in motion as a queen's chin,
the ordinary toes carrying cautiously every ocellate
moon, sun, whorl, enjambment of color.

The waterlily cups have unclenched to the light:
white and pink still chilly, ixora and oleander
moist still: but the Mexican sun is stoked and ready.
The peacock mixes blues and greens, deepens them, pauses,
preparing to celebrate himself in an invisible glass
that kindles a blue royal enough for a *pavo real*.

You, a woman not dazzling, and cripplingly caught,
moved as swift and pitiless as light, neither less nor more,
among the pinchbeck vanities, the mingy shifts
of the heart, the small shabby panics of the killer,
the lethal state of grace abrupt as a pitfall.
Intellect, intellect, love and shame occupied your power.

Yet the stupid, vain, ill-tempered peacock obsessed
                                        your desire
from child to death: the unfurled arc
the eye of glory, the tilted head of a bad bird,
went straight to the center spot, the bullseye of mystery:
its maker's pleasure in a living thing
lovely and loveless as a pausing peacock

who pauses now, suddenly to hoist his soundless plumes
trembling and blazing in a fringy arc:
to the right he bows his crest; shudders his moons;
ignited by the sun, bows to the left.
That message of gratuitous pleasure, to the beholder,
in communion with our joy transfixed you.

THE CLASS

The small black blobs on the beach are the heads
of children. Defectives:
the imbeciles could not come, and the morons
have graduated to lives.
Five sit under the sun at the tide's edge.

Everything moves: like a motion of silence a sailboat
goes on the sea's brilliant shiver;
the glittery palms make the sound of raining,
clouds change shape, waves curl over.
The five stay still as five struck in one pose.

They are out for an outing in the free great air:
they face the Caribbean;
the air will not bear them up, nor the sea,
nor the sand grow an herb to heal,
nor the thick white clouds transport them elsewhere.

This is no lesson the voice gives.
They listen, listen in a secret school,
their faces lifted: conscienceless, on their skin
the tongue of the tide says, *Cool . . .*
and in glazed brightness the sun says, *Live . . .*

IN THE CREVICE OF TIME

FOR ELLIOTT COLEMAN

The bison, or tiger, or whatever beast
hunting or hunted, and the twiggy hunter
with legs and spear, in the still caves of Spain
wore out the million rains of summer
and the mean mists of winter:
the frightening motion of the hunter-priest

who straight in the instant between blood and breath
saw frozen there not shank or horn or hide
but an arrangement of these by him, and he himself
there with them, watched by himself inside
the terrible functionless whole
in an offering strange as some new kind of death.

The thick gross early form that made a grave
said in one gesture, "neither bird nor leaf."
The news no animal need bear was out:
the knowledge of death, and time the wicked thief,
and the prompt monster of foreseeable grief:
it was the tentative gesture that he gave.

Our hulking confrère scraping the wall,
piling the dust over the motionless face:
in the abyss of time how he is close,
his art an act of faith, his grave
an act of art: for all,
for all, a celebration and a burial.

THE LOVERS

The lovers lie in the shelter of night, the lovers
lie in each other's arms in night's crux:
the clock stopped and stars still and fire
unlit, in each other's arms lie the lovers.

Still clock and stopped stars are not true:
cold dust blows from the stars, cold iron roars
through space, time ticks trapped in the two
lovers' wrists. False, stopped clock and still stars.

On the cold hearth, to kindle the lovers' fire,
stuffed under logs lie inky rage and retribution;
on a nail on the wall, stretched arms and folded feet
hang and motionlessly reproduce an execution.

Here the stars make no sound, there is no wind, no clock.
Once an animal cried out in the tall cold meadow
grass, beyond the glass cried out, addressing owl or fox.
Who will stay the lovers in their single shadow?

The lovers lie in the shelter of their deaths;
though they move, now, to part, it is a feint at most:
who were two have died, and are safe in a single breath:
they are discovered, found with all the lost.

THE MOON WILL RESTORE
THE VIRGINITY OF MY SISTER

Camino Real

Over my paws
the violet lids are lowered, the varnished wasp's nest
bowed; the dial on her pulse flays her away
to tininess; the manicure is half over, the day
is half over, her life.

The silver talons flash on the small hard fingers.
No ring on the left hand, on the right
a ring the size of a mouse;
at the eyes' corners, over the lovely bones,
the reassembled waitings have put prints. The channel of
                                                    her hope
curves back very far.
Chanel says she is a flower, as the silver nails
say she is lunar. O prepared, prepared
for the waited stranger's desire
encouraged this dark day early in the hostile glass.

She flips her towel and rolls her rosy vial
warming in palms her sacred senseless hope.
Over my nails' half-moons, bent like Picasso,
with catquick licks she paints my forty fingers.

MY SMALL AUNT

died in a dust of lions; her Africa
was secret as her body and arrived
like the biblical robber by night, by darkest night;
that night, however, was the cinema's:
where there before her, high and bright, and wide
as love, it stretched its radiant sinister light.
And by the foreground clump of pampas grass
shone the pride.

She knew it all before she saw it all.
Light-hearted as a warrior come home
she absolved its horrors: the bald-neck buzzards,
carrion-content; and in the waterhole
the gross great pigs that float their eyes on scum;
the cough, the red snatched meal, the hot-breathed hazard;
in what sense the pride goeth before the fall—
the hunted one.

Was she the hunter or the hunted? Both.
At home, the click and tick of cup and clock
failed to falter in any changes. Hunted
by pain, and tireless hunter of the moth,
she turned no key within a useless lock.
No nephew, nay, no friend, went disappointed.
But in her sun slept lions, chockablock
with blood and sloth.

She queued for her ticket in the stale winter street,
and, step for step, the mean wind cried like a ghoul
in her ear and flourished its trash and her blue eye wept.
But closer and close, the aromatic heat
and the flat trees; and like a homing soul
she met the spaces the hot grasses kept
and met the motion of four soundless feet:
the paced prowl.

Hunted or hunter. Too brave to be sad,
the fear of pity fixed her like a stare.
Sharp starry hunters, luminous orions
whirled in her sleep. Taking her cup in bed
she drank unsweetened courage black and clear.
In their gold ruffs waited the shining lions,
violent and sunny lords who never had
pity or fear.

SECTION

. . . had arranged
to pick her
up, at the flower-show, but there
he found arrangements
using live flowers
that never made a sound: and where
exactly was she among
the gimlet-eyed daffodil growers?

As he passed,
the petals set off metals
and fangs, shards, glass;
and the stalk of her body
when he saw it
bore up on another arrangement a petal
face: this arrangement had proportion,
scale, and definitely theme.
Nothing, no, nothing stirred: root, soil,
sap, breeze, bees:
what on earth of earth
could come through it, he said,
seeing it propped for him
on its snapped stem.

THE MATADORS

The dirty money and the sleazy hearts
swell the *fiesta brava;*
in cheap *sol,* dear *sombra,* sit the greedy
strong-armed with expendable cokes and cushions-
missile-rebukes of buyers to the bought:

pig-eyed, big-assed, the princes of peseta,
tycoon of horses, tycoon of *billetes,*
knowers of the greasy ropes, the skid;
aficionados of the tide that turns:

the bloodshock of the trumpets,
the celestial suit, the very sand
under the sole of the slipper
crying, what is sold a man
if he lose his profit?

Yet it is silly to say
that their blood and their wrists have not spoken,
the fighters with names like lights:
El Espartaro, Manolete, Josalito.
They speak to us.

The bulls were always there;
in the moonlight pastures,
moving through the shadows
the blacker shadows.

They speak,
the matadors. To us.
Right-thinking cannot hush
them, nor the crowds, their enemy;
nor the gentle wish.

39

They will speak and we will answer.
Unless someone is born
who has not set himself
before the dark horned shape

alone,
set his feet in sand
calling softly, hoarsely,
Toro, toro! Venga!

THE INTERRUPTED

Of the goddess there is only the marble shoulder and one
keen breast, lifted in a shout or love.
The axle is all that remains of the race.

On the smashed frieze, the forelegs, jubilant,
spring from no stallion: spring in the glass case
under the shadow of outside almond bloom.

On a stump, leafless, the slender headless youth
leans on his elbow, tenderly in stone,
to watch something in absence.

Acanthus cannot shake, though wind from the sea comes in:
the acanthus is a scrap from a scrap of column.
It is stopped short and waits for us.

The noble plunge of the stallion, the race, the shout,
the eyes' view, the acanthus moved by the wind
achieve themselves in this stone room—

of the company of their unbroken peers, the lords.
These escape from their maker's limit to rejoice us
with hope. These are the interrupted.

41

ARRIVAL

Up the path, past the iced birdbath and the black roses;
the street black, too. But the lamp at the door
shows the face: forbidden, totally forbidden.
Over the threshold. And downstairs the door unmistakably
                                        closes.

The only forbidden face, actually, truly forbidden: bare,
narrow and intent, colder than the yard's clay.
His intentions are intimate, no question of that.
He is not, in point of fact, hurrying, but has reached
                                        the turn in the stair.

Perhaps a brief visit? The disastrous and not-necessarily-fatal
                                        feet
are here and a knob turns. A sandwich perhaps, in a
                                        cardboard box?
A shared midnight snack? A thick suitcase in either hand?
Or is there a van, huge in the invisible street?

ON MY ISLAND

they kill mongooses. Always, before they club
the trapped head, a formal greeting is offered:
"Good morning, Mr. Mongoose."
If they struck in silence, a sharp-toothed shade
would come for them: feral, affronted
to have been anonymous, unidentified,
unsaluted. After good morning and the courteous
title, if not the beast, his spirit, is appeased.

A man as murderer explained his situation's
anonymity: They didn't say, man, he said,
or woman, or child: he said, they just said
dead mongooses—no, communists. They didn't
say anything about age, or anything. So he never
thought to say, Good morning,
child.

DESTINATIONS

Home is mysterious: a place to die, a place to breed;
a rock, a streambed, a burrow. From far far far,
a deadly magnet: violent, unarguable rapid need.

The wastes of waters, the printless wastes of air, prepare
for them death, failure, but never death of destination—
the thread snapped off in the labyrinth, the shifting
                                        of a star.

From the Brazilian water-pastures, in her homing passion
the green turtle travels fourteen hundred miles to find
(with tiny water-level eye) Ascension Island reared above
                                        her motion.

Eels. No eel in the west world but is reminded
in autumn of Sargasso; to its weeds and washes comes
                                        in spring
to breed, and to die: the elvers will return to do in kind.

The Manx shearwater (monogamous as a wolf) flying
back back to his unidentifiable cliffy burrow; the albatross,
the salmon: need I labor the point in fur, fin, wing?

The point is established. But if I swim, I sink, if I fly,
                                        I fall.
How do I then know that over the terrible distances
                        where you are, I must arrive?

The point is established. But the how, the how is not
                                        established at all.

But there is a question below the question of how I contrive
finally to reach you through the disasters of my weather.
I must come, and I come; so I accede, prevail, arrive.

44

But we are tricked. O most fortunate fin and feather,
fortunate voyagers, come where you had to go.
Now it turns out that this was a shelter, a shelter we
                                        leave together
for elsewhere: and the shadows pulsing say *night* and
                            the short wind says *snow*.

GHOSTS AT KHE SANH

Under the bullets
the babies of the Sioux tumble
the babies crumple like clay;
the squaws stumble and try to crawl.
The wigwams blaze like comets;
in the snow the children fall, painting it.

Their ghosts blow like smoke over Khe Sanh,
ghost to familiar ghost:
the huts burn like shabby suns:
the sons and daughters lie
where they fell running.
The women cannot move to touch,
before they join
the confused, blowing ghosts.

Over the ditch air is full of ghosts
given up.
Is it a prairie, snowy wood,
or paddy field and dust, to dust? Where is its name?
How shall we tell?
The faces, the faces of the strangers are the same.

INSOMNIAC'S BIRD

The first clear faint unlocated call
through the whole dark reaches the ear.
At that, the gothic shapes of guilt and doom break stride;
the hard obsessive patter of the detail
hot on the naked heel, the hours' coil,
the pulsing pause that is neither there, nor here,

collapse. Light will define the fringes of the fern;
the bird will bring it and the grass will deepen it.
O the good stir and rumor. You can go
now into its promise, as the dark tide turns,
stranding the hulk of apple trees and barn,
floating stars westward. Therefore, waker, sleep.

Waker, though the soaked fields lie without a sound,
since that single note, feel how the dark is crazed
like a plate; and what far fire did that, will come
to show green, grown out of the sightless ground,
wings trust air, and fingers form their hand.
Now is the act of sleep quick, true and easy.

NOTES FROM A LENTEN BAR

I know that my redeemer liveth because
the pebble-eyed gent with the briefcase
two tables down has called him by name
3 times in 2 and ¾ minutes;
and because
the guys on my right are liquid with the health
of victorious Immaculate Conception, 46 to 98;
and because
after the last of my supper, I learn once more
as I rise to 1403
there is nothing between the 12th and the 14th floor.

BUSH CHRISTMAS EVE

FOR JOE GALLAGHER

In the pictures, the crèche,
the animals were there, but mild.
I have seen the moon in blackness
light the green jelly of Hyena's eye;

seen Crocodile, while something tells
the oldest coldest jest
that keeps its savor,
smiling, listen.

Saviour, I never saw you painted
flanked by those eyes, that grin.
I paint you there, tonight.
Well, in any case, Come.

Welcome. I cannot bless
that green, that grin.
You who imagined them, bless
them by coming.

And since I bless
your coming, why, I praise
and bless what you imagined,
with you between them.
Only come.

WHEN THE FIVE PROMINENT POETS

gathered in inter-admiration
in a small hotel room, to listen
to each other, like Mme. Verdurin
made ill by ecstasy,
they dropped the Muse's name.
Who came.

It was awful.
The door in shivers and a path
plowed like a twister through everything.
Eyeballs and fingers littered that room.
When the floor exploded the ceiling
parted
and the Muse went on and up; and not a sound
came from the savage carpet.

BUSH

It is the sound of lions lapping.
They drink themselves
from the gold shapes that waver
and grow shallower.

Blue peels itself in the water-
hole; it is the sun coming.
Crouched, the lions meet
their matches at the surface.

The foxy jackals are far off
but the vultures cloud the flat treetop;
the drum of the zebra's body
is lined with red sunrise.

The jackals and vultures are waiting
for what happened under the moon.
The lions are through with it; they
lift their dripping chins and look ahead.

It is six o'clock on Christmas morning.
Now the lions have stopped lapping
the bush makes no sound
the vultures shift, but without sound.

The day is perfectly seamless.
Slowly the lions move like pistons past the dry grasses;
the jackals do not move yet;
the vultures show patience.

The lions pass a thornbush and melt.
Though the whole day is unbroken
the passage of the sun will represent heaven;
the bones will represent time.

GENTLE READER

Late in the night when I should be asleep
under the city stars in a small room
I read a poet. A poet: not
a versifier. Not a hot-shot
ethic-monger, laying about
him; not a diary of lying
about in cruel cruel beds, crying.
A poet, dangerous and steep.

O God, it peels me, juices me like a press;
this poetry drinks me, eats me, gut and marrow
until I exist in its jester's sorrow,
until my juices feed a savage sight
that runs along the lines, bright
as beasts' eyes. The rubble splays to dust:
city, book, bed, leaving my ear's lust
saying like Molly, yes, yes, yes O yes.

THE PLANET

FOR ERLEND

From the center of the Sea of Tranquility—
a dry sea and a grainy—
see shining on the air
of that stretched night, a planet.

See it as serene and bright, very bright,
a far fair neighbor;
conceive what might be there
after the furious spaces.

Green fields, green fields,
oceans of grasses, breakers of daisies;
shadows on those fields,
vast and traveling,

the clouds' shadows.
And something smaller:
in the green grass, lovers in each other's
arms, still, in the grass.

The clouds will water the fields
the stream run shining
to the sea's motion; the sea shining
as the clouds travel and shine,

so shine the daisies, as
the light in the seas
of the lovers' eyes. The innocent planet
far and simple, simple because far:

with lovers, and fields for flowers,
and a blue sky carrying clouds;
and water, water: the innocent planet,
shining and shining.

From LET EACH MAN REMEMBER

MAN AND THE LION

The yellow lion shakes the ground—
Hunting the range which is his choice—
By the great pulse of his profound
And savage voice.

But man confronts, with halted stride
Of twiggy legs, the hot eyeballs
Of the caged cat, and notes with pride
That its gaze falls.

The golden lion of the sun
Starting across the lucent sky
Makes no attempt to catch and stun
The human eye.

Yet, as the mole which shelters in
The grubby and protective dark,
We burrow, when the hunt begins,
Lest we be mark

For the terrible light. How can our spirit
Endure this overheaping measure
Of shame, until we shall inherit
Celestial pleasure

To watch the sun appease his wrath
With glut of stars—the lovely Seven,
The moon—as he crosses on his path
The lit heaven?

LET EACH MAN REMEMBER

There is a terrible hour in the early morning
When men awake and look on the day that brings
The hateful adventure, approaching with no less certainty
Than the light that grows, the untroubled bird that sings.

It does not matter what we have to consider,
Whether the difficult word, or the surgeon's knife,
The last silver goblet to pawn, or the fatal letter,
Or the prospect of going on with a particular life.

The point is, they rise; always they seem to have risen,
(They always will rise, I suppose) by courage alone.
Somehow, by this or by that, they engender courage,
Courage bred in flesh that is sick to the bone.

Each in his fashion, they compass their set intent
To rout the reluctant sword from the gripping sheath,
By thinking, perhaps, upon the Blessed Sacrament,
Or perhaps by coffee, or perhaps by gritted teeth.

It is indisputable that some turn solemn or savage,
While others have found it serves them best to be glib,
When they inwardly lean and listen, listen for courage,
That bitter and curious thing beneath the rib.

With nothing to gain, perhaps, and no sane reason
To put up a fight, they grip and hang by the thread
As fierce and still as a swinging threatened spider.
They are too brave to say, It is simpler to be dead.

Let each man remember, who opens his eyes to that morning,
How many men have braced them to meet the light,
And pious or ribald, one way or another, how many
Will smile in its face, when he is at peace in the night.

RESIDUE

Best, without doubt, is deed,
easing the breath;
Triumph, if it succeed,
And if not, death.

But the hands, to confound,
Must touch and take;
Some hands there are
Tight to the stake.

Yet grows beneath this mesh
Coward to fire,
Beneath this accessible flesh,
The iron desire:

Valor of the oppressed,
Victory. Still,
Under too savage test
Crumples the will.

What then is left beyond
Dust, ash and shame?
Honor dead, and the bond,
As a dead flame?

The knowledge and its seed—
The heart's, the brain's—
Beneath the flesh, and deed,
And will, this remains.

This shall suffice alone:
More wise than hell,
Of heaven the pith and stone,
This, indestructible.

MARK THEN THE BREATH

In modern semblance of
St. Francis and King Nero,
Passes below, above,
The criminal or hero.

The eager waiting eyes
Find succor in the sight
Of him who forged the lies
And him who struck the light.

When on the balcony
Celestial in the sun
The man has stood so high
That worship has begun

And then the traitorous truth
Disclose him for a knave
Whom all had held in sooth
The blessed and the brave,

Mark then the lifting breath—
Exultant to destroy,
Silent but cruel as death—
Of a tumultuous joy.

When in the narrow street
Naked of shade or friend,
Pass the reluctant feet
To harsh and certain end,

If through the crowd there burst
Messenger of defense
Bearing to the accursed
Proof of his innocence,

The hot, incredulous breath
Catches; desire, maimed,
Seeks the expected death,
Angry and unashamed;

Mark how the sullen cloud
Shadows the breathless day:
Here the immobile crowd,
There the escaping prey.

IN ISOLATION

When at a desperate plight
His sentience quits its mesh
To taste the acrid fright
Within the alien flesh,

To know the separate pain
Which is no piece of his,
Almost a man may gain
Identity in this.

Almost he may believe
He has worked miracle
And does in fact conceive
An unfamiliar hell;

Almost he shall descry
The small and dreadful day
From which he cannot fly
Because there is no way:

Almost he has escaped
Ego's lonely law;
Here are two halves, twin-shaped,
Divided by a straw.

Just at identity,
Just as the perfect tone,
Suddenly he is free—
Suddenly it is lost . . . gone.

Once more descends the chill
The healthy life has shunned
Where move in secret still
The sad and moribund.

From artificial care
Fostered beyond its scope,
Goes up the stranger's prayer,
The insulated hope.

WHO SHALL ESCAPE THE LORD?

If he be agile and alert
A man may baffle many a hurt;
If he be merry and aware
A man shall mock at many a snare.

But though he guard his continence
From siege without and hot offense,
Though he be shrewd to save his skin
How shall he quit the foe within?

For no more shall escape a man
From this assault than fly he can
By any sudden turn or twist
The bright blood pounding in his wrist.

He still shall carry on his flight,
Unrecognized, his curious plight:
Within the core, without a name,
The ineradicable flame.

FEBRUARY MIDNIGHT

No sheltered ear can miss,
Though stalwart be the wall,
At midnight such as this,
The homeless faint footfall.

The kindly man shall sigh
And feed the friendly flame
And valiantly deny
The small and fierce shame;

The poet's heart shall burn
Until he form a verse
When he shall sigh and turn
And slumber none the worse;

The woman warm in love
Shall find her mind possessed
Now by the rigor of
An uninvited guest,

And sharply start away
From what she might discover
And seek in mute dismay
The body of her lover.

Only the hermit's breath
Frosted upon the air,
Incognizant of death
And conqueror of despair,

Through poverty's sweet ease
Immune from pity's rod,
Shall hold in scatheless peace
Its intercourse with God.

IMMORTAL ELEMENT

The watching inner eye that peers and sees
The lovely accident, the curious texture
Apart from place and content, wisely knows
The valid tint in the confusing mixture.

The gaze is not irrelevant, which notes
In the rope's coil, design instead of noose,
Or how the murderous water takes the lights,
Or, at a terrible moment, the enemy's grace.

It does not wander foolishly—assured
That though the purpose conquer, there shall rest
finally preserved, only the element bared
By this impersonal sight, released at last.

HOLIDAY

He lived with Sorrow, protected by his Will.
For fear he might arouse
The hulking giant, he never crossed that sill.
The three shared house.

He dreamed sometimes the giant had wrenched loose
His terrible strong hands;
And then he watched the slim lithe Will, by ruse
Testing the bands.

So lightly he went up and down the stairs,
Merry enough, and free,
Thinking they made a friendly, gallant pair,
The Will and he.

One day the Will, who had grown strained and thin,
Wearied of playing groom,
Took holiday, and left him idle in
An upper room

(Having first visited and double-barred
The darkened lower floor).
He felt afraid, and went and listened hard
At his closed door,

And sure enough, there came a clank and rattle,
Then stillness, dead;
Then, mixed with curses and the crazy prattle,
A mounting tread.

THE QUEEN'S SONGS

I

The skies are falling and poised in their fall,
The earth is riven beneath our feet,
The stars like birds with lost shrill call
Swirl in the air where thunders beat.

The sea is swelling, the somber tide
Darkly arisen, towers above
Our tiny heads, and the light has died—
Here is the crevice and foothold of love.

The mad earth plunges through the night
But we lie here in a small still space,
Here, in the core of the furious flight,
Body to body, and face to face.

From FOR THE UNLOST

ESCAPE IN ICE

We have forgotten weather, by virtue of the protecting mass
Of wall. We may remark the voice of January in the eaves,
Or a blue-and-green May day, blowing over, beyond the glass,
But they are neither kind nor cruel, the ice, the leaves.

On a day this winter our lives were minutely altered—
The lanes were bright and smooth as the clicking branches
of trees,
All was touched by a giant finger—the inexorable rhythm
faltered,
And ice and wind became larger, and real, and we were
captive of these.

Men kept at home, there was no school, the children curled
By the fire and people spoke in a special voice;
The tides and winds and seasons of the ancient world
Were again in power for a moment, and the heart could
in secret rejoice

In the glittering pause, in the old recurrence,
that discovers
To men nervous with power, the helpless escape.
The fierce weather
Is master; all life is in the small warm room. And the lovers
Stare through blind windows and laugh, and come together.

TERRESTRIAL

This day was made of dust,
The bright and lovely
And utterly perishing—
Nothing that we could trust, nothing worth cherishing.

No skeleton to stay and whiten,
No soul to escape—
The word was *never,*
Nothing like *love,* to frighten; dust, lost forever.

Moss, rainbow rock, fall apart,
The cold pools vanish
Without resurrection.
The alien human heart, strange to perfection

Understands this, its own:
Not past, not future,
Not truth, to enmesh us—
This was our dust alone, O ours, O precious.

SPRING, SAYS THE CHILD

There are words too ancient to be said by the lips of a child—
Too old, too old for a child's soft reckoning;
Ancient, terrible words, to a race unreconciled:
Death, spring . . .

The composite heart of man knows their awful age—
They are frightening words to hear on a child's quick tongue.
They overshadow, with their centuries' heritage
The tenderly young.

Death, says the child, *spring,* says the child, and *heaven . . .*
This is flesh against stone, warm hope against salt sea—
This is all things soft, young, ignorant; this is even
Mortality.

FOR WILFRED OWEN

This day, this night, should be familiar to you,
These sounds, these faces, this red mud and glare;
Again is served, upon the board that knew you,
The ugly feast at which you took your share.

The skeletons at ease beneath the crosses
Are unconcerned with diving Messerschmitts,
Impervious to estimated losses
And unambitious of director hits.

They, safe as you, ignore delirium;
This time your lips escape the bitter ration
And the sick stumbling men whose lips are dumb
Go scatheless from your terrible compassion.

FOR THOSE WHO HAVE NOT
EATEN THE APPLE

The unclosing flowers are inflexible and have yielded nothing,
At the tree's base the hairy grass is strong and green,
And there is an ignorance of guilt, of weariness; a breathing
Of uncomplicated air, as in some pre-apple Eden.

This is innocence: it dwells in savage children,
In unreflecting men cleaning the valves, in the birds'
Tempestuous blood; it cannot understand the hidden
Meaning of good. It is too fresh for the word's age.

This is alluring: it is the scathelessness of the new,
The stiffness of virgin cloth, the motion of young men;
It is the gift of the child, it is cold and clear, like dew,
Calling not for admiration but certainly for envy.

ARDENT SALUTE

To the man in the core of the flame,
Luck, and the waiting eyes—
Breath stopped at what he does,
Hope held, when hope should be gone.

To the man in the usual hours
Such merit as may be;
In simple necessity
We shall respect life's share.

To the donor of others' youth—
Couch-fretter after raid,
Desk-devotee of blood—
Contempt, like a blow in the mouth.

MIDNIGHT TREE

The crusted tree of stars soars quite
Across the sky,
Mammoth, unstirred, stiff with a bright
Rigidity.

The branches glitter, forked and still
In the great air,
Distant, enormous, by midnight visible
And very fair.

The Tree, the Tree, lovely and not for us;
With light for wood
It grows, as ever, desired, dangerous,
Not understood.

FOR A DANCER

FOR WALTER SORELL

Paint bites deep
And will last your day
And then beyond it, a century.

Marble will stop
When empires burn;
It will wait in the ground the cold spade's turn.

What melody
Is kin to the flesh?
It is yours no more than a wind or a wish.

But this has the mark
Of such as we;
This is the art of mortality.

This is our own
As never another;
The link of the stone and the note with the feather.

Ancient and true—
But weightless as foam,
And gone with the dancer as heat with the flame.

LINES TO A POET

Be careful what you say to us now.
The street-lamp is smashed, the window is jagged,
There is a man dead in his blood by the base of the fountain.
If you speak
You cannot be delicate or sad or clever.
Some other hour, in a moist April,
We will consider similes for the budding larches.
You can teach our wits and our fancy then;
By a green-lit midnight in your study
We will delve in your sparkling rock.
But now at dreadful high noon
You may speak only to our heart,
Our honor and our need:
Saying such things as, "See, she is alive . . ."
Or "Here is water," or "Look behind you!"

From THE HUMAN CLIMATE

GUIDE FOR SURVIVORS

First comes the flight, of course. Hope gleams in steel
And lean tracks flash and conjugate the hope:
"I shall escape," "I will escape!" even "I am
Escaping"; and the salty prow repeats
In a soft rush "seascape, safe cape, escape."
Station and quay support him, porter, taxi—
Timid but trustful through the alien air
To the red reassurance of the lobby.
Pages and aspidistras take him in.
The bedroom door flies back and windowed there
Clash palms, burns bay, felicitous and fresh
With all the tonic tropic of delight.

And only when the blue boy has withdrawn,
His hat on the bed, ice water at his lips,
Do his eyes meet the eyes in the far corner
Where the squat figure has awaited him.

At this, far too intelligent to flee,
He knows that hope now lies in strategy
And carefully returns to ancient use.
Monsters can mope, and lonely monsters leave.
At midnight, shimmering under falling notes
Faces of friends like flowers in a rain
Shine fresh as truth and laughter crests and breaks.
His covert gaze, ranging the rustling room,
Finds out no undesired watching thing;
Best, when the door has closed on him again
With curded smoke and petals dropped on glass,
The place is his. Till, leaning on the mantel,
Who was not there before, regards him, speechless.

Pure terror has him now; now he perceives
The visitor is at home.

In the back room
He holds destruction neatly in his palm,
Small, cold, and practical, and marvels briefly
Upon how death, that democratic lord,
Can be commanded like a ready lackey
By a crooked finger. But he does not crook it.

Some root of joy, some subterranean pride
Feeds him his strength again in slow sharp drops,
And strength restores him to the outer room.
Keeping his eyes upon the watching face
He does not hope to alienate or fly,
He mentions gravely the inclement night,
Fetches a blanket for the couch. And then
The worst befalls—the face profoundly changes
To friendship sudden as love.

THE INNOCENTS

The faces of children turn like sunflowers to death;
With popcorn and attention they defer
To the ditch-dead woman snuffed by the timid cur,
The sudden soldier spinning on the beach.

(Raped from the roses, from the summer core,
From the cool parlor with the peacock feathers
To this dark shrine that miracles all weathers
All oceans and all foreignness to here.)

The guilty adults watch the faces turn
Uplifted to the toadstool of disaster
That rears before them bigger faster vaster
Than any cautious parent made them learn;

The guilty adults watch with guilty eyes
The peacock-feather vase; locked from the garden
Weep penance for themselves and find no pardon
For this deflowering—and cannot see

The awkward lady with the queer eye sockets,
The funny airman dropping like a swallow;
The terrible peacock-eyes that seem to follow;
The striped rage of the monstrous yellow jacket.

THEY NEVER WERE FOUND

The odd, the inward-turned, the isolated:
The old gent who raises cats in his bedroom;
(A bright-eyed folk, quick through the doors
And made happy by fish);
Mr. Fleet who converses with his dead daughter
Over boiled milk on the kitchen range at midnight;
The elderly lady in a sailor hat
Who rides a scooter to the bank
From which she withdraws a little—only a very little.
She has a fat and shining balance in that bank
On the day when, the milk being accumulated,
Neighbors force the lock:
The air bad, no furniture, but three great piles of rubbish;
On the third, the mistress of the house, quite dead
                                        by starving.

This was their fort-life, beleaguered, unallied—
One by his stove,
One on her scooter,
One in the dangerous company of his cats.

THE LIMIT ESCAPED

FOR BILL MUELLER

Forewarned by wit, the approach is shallow,
Aware of rock submerged, of sudden ground
Where the diver was sure no impact would follow,
Hoped for profound depths to pierce.

The time varies slightly, but is always reached
As in art, love, in physical pleasure,
When the familiar brimming moment is approached:
When the measure suddenly will hold no more.

Then, fierce with need, as an angry comet
Will have space more space for flight in the sky,
As strangled lungs seek for air without limit
And the blinded eye will have all color,

God is sought, to sink in, to rush through.
The deadly limit, the bond, is eluded, escaped;
For a moment at most, for the space of a thought at worst
Is possessed the shape of utter freedom.

VARIATIONS ON VARIETY

1. Comic

Conservative heart, outdone by all upheaval,
Let solid laughter, greeting the emergence
Of stooge and comic from the wings, set free
Your fear from troubled dreams of anarchy:
These point the norm by patter of divergence.

Semple and Simple, in costume as in concept,
Bank on the ancient budget of surprise:
The strength of midget, lewdness of duenna,
The slipping pants, the skin of the banana,
Rest on the pattern where all these are lies.

To a thousand minds, the traveling-salesman gag
Supports the marble niche of chastity
(Presupposition of the two-a-day)
As each round penny of the juggler's pay
Supports the unsmiling rule of gravity.

2. Tight-rope Walker

The bright-check suited
Walks—our hope—
To music, muted,
The vibrant rope.

In a sliding dance
He moves to measure;
Our life, in balance,
Our swaying treasure.

With redglow gaze
Watch the evil three;
Vertigo, praise
And gravity.

To their shame, to their rage
At the other side
He has leaped to the stage,
He is bowing, our pride.

This is sweet which we shared:
He has justified men;
We are puny, we dared,
We have balanced again.

3. Sister Act

Red, blue and green, the Murphy sisters sing,
                          and interstellar space
Has not frightened their scintillant, sequined trio
                    from the sycophant microphone
That dulcetly magnifies murmurs; and they are—
                heads together casual arm about waist—
On a stage in a city in a country on a continent, superbly at
                                    home.

Street lamp, façade and alley, slum, urban garden
                          and plaza and boulevard
Lie, wrapped and reassuring, round them, then
                          Maryland hills and water
And wide wide to the west rolling under the moonlight
                          that enormous word
America; but a word like oceans is bigger and colder
                              and weightier.

86

The hanging hemispheres, the pendent water caught back
                                          from its fall,
Stand them in stead; three undismayed, not given to brooding
                                          vainly;
The baby-spot clasps them, so that the spinning tiny star in its
                                          well
Of black winds rushing through space, of nothing and
                    nowhere and none, shall not make them lonely.

Green, blue and red, they are able to take an encore
                              with an ending soft and high,
For terror will not open upon them like a door with an oiled
                                          hinge.
They can bow like jonquils—for the mind will not step to
                    their shoulder, and succinct and wicked, betray
The device spread over thin space, the tissue paper between
                              the foot and the plunge.

BALLAD OF HENRY, BRIDEGROOM

Henry of England could pray or roister,
He had power and youth and some acumen;
The world, indeed, was Henry's oyster—
But this is the ballad of man and woman.
He was strong and proud and his wrath was red.
Comes the day when the quick are the dead,
Christ have mercy when we are sped.

Catherine's pride was tortured and white
But stiff as the bone of Aragon—
Alien queen who could suffer and fight
But never could rear an English son.
"One flesh till death," Spanish Catherine said.
Comes the day when the quick are the dead,
Christ have mercy when we are sped.

The barge was burnished, the roof was gold,
The cannon spoke for the bright newcomer;
Pelted with blossoms, fair and bold
Ann rode the burning Thames of summer.
Nan Bullen had a shining head.
Comes the day when the quick are the dead,
Christ have mercy when we are sped.

Jane, you followed a bloody ghost
Who had been loved, if kings can love;
Henry at last lay by your dust,
Whatever this wish of his may prove.
Jane was honest as salt or bread.
Comes the day when the quick are the dead,
Christ have mercy when we are sped.

Anne of Cleves was a sorry sequel
And doubtless a shock to a bridegroom who
Had been told that her beauty knew no equal
And found this something undertrue.
Henry and Anne kept a virgin's bed.
Comes the day when the quick are the dead,
Christ have mercy when we are sped.

Henry's sense of royal decorum
Found Catherine Howard's virtue lax;
Thomas Culpeper, Francis Dereham
Paid by the rope, and his queen by the axe.
The three were young and nobly bred.
Comes the day when the quick are the dead,
Christ have mercy when we are sped.

Catherine seemed hardly a name for luck,
Nor this elevation a thing to seek;
Catherine Parr, when the long-due struck,
Your distinction remains unique:
You abode when your master fled.
Comes the day when the quick are the dead,
Christ have mercy when we are sped.

The word that pleased him least, was *wife,*
The word writ deep in his heart was *nation;*
He had lively faith in the afterlife,
Probably mixed with trepidation.
What speech holds the king with these he wed
Now in the day when the quick are the dead?
Christ have mercy when we are sped.

MOURNER BETRAYED

He trusted death when it said "I am the end!
Nothing exists now!" But the truth
Seemed that the creeping June-green growth
Covers the face of death and does not mind.

The sun is savage, the grass powerful—
The orchard scents and shadows filter
Into his mind where death sought shelter . . .
He gives it, in his harried heart, a lull.

"Death!" says the heart, grim as a hard-pressed fencer,
"Death the implacable, death the forever!"
But the white May-clouds in stillness travel over
And the fierce dandelions do not answer.

COLLOQUY

"Why? Tell me why!" he said in dismay to Corrigan,
"Should happiness, golden happiness, the profound, the acute,
Be speechless, be dumb; be the song, be the poem of no man,
Silent as the mermaid, as the broken nightingale,
                                    as all the mute?

Out of the dark of centuries, the accents of sorrow break,
From antiquity full and generous, without stint or ration:
From the loss of love, from the waste spaces, from the
                                    candescent stake,
Comes articulate music—the word's memorable passion.

I will have speech for my happiness," he said doggedly,
                                    "speech that is fit
 Now while it is full of strength, while it is fierce and young!"
"And did you think," said Corrigan, "that the Watchers
                                    had not spoken for it?
Did you think that the Watchers of happiness had not
                                    given it tongue?

Are the deep voices pitched too low for your ear,
                                    under the rain
Lashing the shelter, the low voices under the howling
                                    weather?
Death patiently saying, 'If I must wait, I must wait,' and pain
Saying to loneliness, 'Tonight they will sleep together.'"

THE BIRDS

FOR JOHN

Corrigan knew that loneliness is the one human passion;
"The bird-voices cry," he said, "each in its ego's tone,
But the theme is the same," he told me, "whatever the
                                        musical fashion:
The cry of a half a thing, divided, and so, alone."

He told me their notes: Vanity cries "I am beautiful,
                                        therefore love me!
I am Rose, Blue, Green! Love me!" thin and high;
And Fear cries, deep from the swamp, "No, no, you do not
                                        love me!
You will injure me!" Corrigan said in the night you can hear
                                        it cry.

"I am severed," cries Passion, "Love me! Unite me!
                                        See, I am severed!"
Crazily crying in the spruces over the unlistening snow,
"See, I am severed! Love me! Unite me!" crazily fevered,
Over and over, Corrigan said, till the cocks crow.

From the maple at noon Wealth cries, "Love me, for I am
                                        rich! Hear! Hear my sum!
(Wealth crying forlornly, "Love me!" under the August heat)
And Power, "Love me, for I can hurt you!" with the sky
                                        like a plum
And the storm in the oaks, "Love me, for I can hurt you!"
                                        he heard it repeat.

And over the orchard-grass, from the apple, the apple
                                        crusted with bloom,
At dawn the lover cries in the mixed and melting dark,
"Love me, for I love you," in the early green gold gloom,
  Crying ". . . for I love you! Love me!" from the dewy bark.

"And from the wood ahead, from the forest behind, in all
                                        weathers,
  And always," said Corrigan, "always by blackness and sun,
                                from the wood, ahead,
The soul, crying to God, 'Love me!' from the thin desperate
                                shelter of feathers,
  'Love me! Love me forever, for I must live!'" Corrigan said.

From THE ANIMAL INSIDE

REINDEER AND ENGINE

The reindeer
fastened to the great round eye
that glares along the
Finnish forest track
runs runs runs runs runs
before that blast of light, will die
but not look back

will not
look back or aside or swerve
into the black tall deep
good dark of the forests of winter
runs runs runs runs runs
from that light that thrust through his brains nerve
its whitehot splinter.

The reindeer
has all the forests of Finland to flee
into, its snowy crows and owlly
hush; but over the icy ties
runs runs runs runs runs
from his white round i-
dée fixe until he dies.

To his west
is wide-as-the-moon, to his right
is deep-as-the-dark, but
lockt to his roaring light
runs runs runs runs runs
the fleeing flagging reindeer
from, into, the cold
                    wheel's
                    night.

WATER

On that hot journey I became aware of water.
At Panajachel the water ran in the strawberry gardens.
Through the dusty hedge, from the path's deep dust, I could
                                      hear water:
It was low-voiced and bright from the hot pipes; and the
                                  fingers of the pickers
were wet and stained and shiny with water and juice;
the small brown girls in red squatted and picked
to this sound, of water that gratified the red warm bumpy
                                            cones.

At the end of the puffs of dust, at the floor of the dust path,
Atitlán; deep, blue; at levels tepid, cool, chill, cold
below the volcanic perfect cone and its tethered cloud;
all morning it mirrored the cone and the cloud,
the wind boiled it after that in cones of its own
hurrying it over drowned Indians, a priest, and other things
older in a secret heap at a depth it has so far not disclosed.

At Acolman the cistern in the center of the courtyard
of the roofless convent held all that blurred in the day's
                                      breath—
what could stir stone and figures of pain and grace but water?
At Morelia the children and fountains jumped, the zocolo's
                                    blown fountains
sprayed the children, the children and fountains played.
But this was the merest blandest brush with water,
its stage effects palmed off on the uninitiate.

I drove through days of a desert blind and cracked and white
with light
and stones, bones, bone stones and limbs of barebone trees;
there were doves, vultures, coyotes; thorns, iguanas, doves,
and the shadows were stunted; the goats traveled in haloes
of dust and slipped on the stones of furnace arroyos.
Once a dusty pair of coyotes leaped down
into a rocky gully and raised a little yellow cloud that floated.

The dusty doves and the muscle-bound vultures rocking
like wrestlers over the split earth toward their feast were
clouded, and everything was silent and yellow with that ghost
of earth:
the sky shone through its haze; the dazed earth gave no dew.
Water was before the eye, in the mind, the ear, the bone,
before the parched lips, on the parched tongue.
All that land hummed like a wire with absent water.

THE STRANGER AND CORRIGAN

I asked Corrigan about the man, alone at the wood's edge,
Who stood in shadow; the motionless stranger.
He did not stir or speak, and he bore in his face and eyes
The marks perhaps of terrible cold and certainly hunger.

I had come through the journey alive, and into the field,
And the sun would have warmed the dead and made them
answer;
And I saw the way he stood, and his coat, and hands.
A stranger returned from this trip is more close
than a brother.

So I spoke the word of the way, and he answered once;
But he never moved or came through the windy flowers.
And I said to Corrigan, "He is one of them
But he will not smile or speak—only watches the mowers.

"The field will be gone," I said, "while he stands and looks—
Tell him I am one—though I went, it is true, in summer."
But Corrigan would not question him and the mowers moved
Bright in the glitter of grasses, toward the newcomer.

"Bitter and strange, I agree, in summer as in winter,
But different in winter. Also," Corrigan said,
"Tell me, when you went, and lived, and returned—
Did you travel alone, and without bread?"

THE SEA FOG

It was sudden.
That slightly heaving hotel, from a folder,
was there one instant: through the glass a bloodorange ball
just diving, a pure blue desert of dusk
on the other horizon: a motion, the symbol of seas;
music, and drinks, and the self-conscious apparel,
the relative facets, of steward and poster, and sun-disc
just hidden.

The ship spoke
with a minotaur sound from around and under
and we raised our eyes: but the sea was gone:
sub-sun, the peel of moon, the plausible shift
of dunes of water, our precious image of movement—
gone, gone, clean gone. The fog was at the pane.
No shore behind us; ahead in the breathy drift
no port.

Supported
by shore and port, now we had neither.
There was only here. The ship was here
in the fog. The ship roared and the fog blotted
us into itself and whirled into its rifts,
and the sealess skyless fear—and there was fear—
had nothing to do with sinking—at least, not
into water.

Worse:
when we went below, at the familiar turn
a bulkhead reared instead, metal and huge—
and trapped, we turned from that hulk and hastened
through stranger stairs and came from a different angle
to a cabin stiller and smaller though none of its objects
                                                    had moved.
But the mirror stirred like fog when we looked for the
                                                    fastened face.

We crept
through fog all night but it closed behind us:
around and very close above:
only below in the black the self-lit fishes
passed ignorantly among the wrack of wrecks
and all the water held its tongue and gave
no password. And so sealed in our silent passage
we slept.

The bell
for the bulkhead doors to open, woke us.
Everything had been reconnected: sun to the sea,
ship to the sun, smiles to our lips, and our names related
to our eyes. Who could—in that brassy blue—
have stillness to harbor the memory
of being relative to nothing; isolated;
responsible?

DEAF-MUTES AT THE BALLGAME

In the hot sun and dazzle of grass
The wind of noise is men's voices:

A torrent of tone, a simmer of roar,
And bats crack, bags break, flags follow themselves.

The hawkers sweat and gleam in the wind of noise,
The tools of ignorance crouch and give the sign.

The deaf-mutes sit in the hurricane's eye,
The shell-shape ear and the useless tongue

Present, but the frantic fingers' pounce-and-bite
Is sound received and uttered.

If they blink their lids—then the whole gaudy circle
With its green heart and ritual figures

Is suddenly not: leaving two animal-quick
Wince-eyed things alone; with masses and masses

And masses of rows of seats of men
Who move their lips and listen.

While secret secret sits inside
Each, his deaf-mute, fingerless.

THE POEM ITSELF

From the ripe silence it exploded silently.
When the bright débris subsided
it was there.

Invisible, inaudible; only
the inky shapes betrayed it.
Betrayed, is the word.

Thence it moved into squalor,
a royal virgin in a brothel,
improbably whole.

It had its followers, pimps, even
its lovers. The man responsible
died, eventually.

When the dust of his brain left the bones
the bond snapped. It escaped to itself.
It no longer answered.

On the shelf, by the clock's tick, in the black
stacks of midnight: it is. A moon
to all its tides.

THE MURMURERS

FOR JOHN GEORGI

They are formidable under any feather
and each name: of fly, of sharp sound, soft sound or flower:
oiseau-mouche, zum-zum, beija-flor—these on the wing.
Their color? Science cries like a lover, of their light:
Heliomaster, Stellula, Chrysolampsis, Sapphira—sun
fire, star fire, torch fire, jewel fire in the air.

Honey, honey—what rapacity: all the air
vibrates with that passion. Ravage, ravage—wing
and beak and raging hunger plunge them, flower by flower,
along the raceme nodding balanced on the light;
the brief immortelle on its yellow great tree of sun,
hog-plum, ixora, wear like a nimbus their fire and feather.

At night, if they wish, they can die; but not quite. Feather-
light, lax, you may handle them, head limp, wing
elegantly shut. But dive up into blue air
at a moment. In 1653 Father Cobo taught the light
of the Resurrection to the Indians by that power. The sun
of their plumage might have served for the Trinity
                                           in flower,

requiring three in one—light, angle, eye, to flower
into their color: lacking one, they go colorless as air.
Interference is the cause of iridescence: feather—
shaft, barb and barbule—must have its sun
as seer; its color is structural, and light
knows this is not a pigment but a murmur of wing.

Water lovers, waterfall lovers, by wet wing
you go, pool shatterers, wet leaf drinkers, light-
ing on nothing: dew drainers, their drenched elected flower
magnetizes metal. Elliptical platelets, feather-
soft? goldsmith stuff inlaid with an eye to air?
Murmurers, feast, fight, flash in the Tobago sun!

Stronger than striped tigers, hotter-blooded, that sun
seethes in their blood: the brilliant obedient air
frees them from patience, fear and commitment. Flower
or hawk they maneuver, the murmurers; by wing, by wing
fight, feast, flash—as though the color's feather
on breast, racket tail, gorget, were an attribute of light.

Songless, belligerent, airy bone and feather,
the round sun like a fruit swells to draw your wing
and needle beak, the whole island's flower is the sound
                                    of your light.

THE ENEMY OF THE HERDS, THE LION*

At Ur
the lady Shub-ad's small
bright box went into the larger darker
shelter of the grave and stayed there roughly
forty-five hundred years.

Its lid—
a sharp arc—shows a thing:
a lion-sheep without division,
lion on top, sheep under, still
consummation point.

The sheep
neck is in the lion fangs
the lion claws press upward the sheep throat, they are
tranced and ardent in act of taking
utter enough to be love.

Back so far
the mind tires on the trip:
so close, the salve or kohl to redden
the lip, lengthen the eye for pleasure's
pleasure, is tonight's.

What is changed?
Not the coarse hairs
of the mane; victor, or victim; a woman's body;
certainly not a death; not the colors
of kohl or scarlet.

* The enemy of the herds, the lion, feeds on its prey on decorated box-lid,
ca. 2500 B.C., which was found in the grave of the Lady Shub-ad at Ur.
Natural History Magazine

She
cared for the box; by wish
expressed or guessed she took it along
as far as might be. Why this one? What
word did her box-beasts mean?

Possi-
bilities; the chic symbols
of the day, on a fashionable jewel-toy,
the owner modishly ignorant; or, corrupt,
an added pulse to lust.

Or:
mocking, or wise, remembrance
of innocent murder innocent death,
the coupled ambiguous desire,
at dinner, at dressing, at music.

Or,
best, and why not? of her meeting
all quiet terror, surmounted by joy,
to go to her grave with her; a pure
mastery older than Ur.

COUNTRY BATH

He was naked in water,
the house all quiet, the raw bulb hanging,
when the great June bug
came booming and crashing
thutter and thutter and soft pop deadly
against the raw brilliance.

Outside the night stared like a monster
million-eyed, gold-eyed, over the mountains;
not a clock-tick, a tap-drip, just
that stutter and thunder.

Then hurt and thrashing and lying and dying
and silence. So he saw
what had only been known; all alone, and at night:
how light

burns.

YELLOW

Yellow became alive.
Materialization took place.
First logically with lemons,
then fresh butter.
Also a chairleg.
After that it appeared
to carve the curve of clouds
and, as sun, shatter them.
The stars grew yellower
yellow whirls on wheels on whirls
leaves flew yellow
the corn sprang
yellow and the crows
winged with a yellow nimbus.
Finally his face
had brilliant yellow
in its grain.
Outside the madhouse hung the yellow sun.

MRS. THROSTLE

Mrs. Throstle said in her garden girdled by meadows and
    mastered by mountains—
    "Here I am close . . ."
by a passion of poppies and white tranced lilac
and the gold-edged breeze-tipped tick ·
    of the petals' time—
    "This is my altar . . ."
the motion of wings and the costly clash
of dewdrops shivered on poppies on lilacs—
    "Here is my temple . . ."
    said Mrs. Throstle.

Where the injured rat is dispatched by the mongrel
the atheist alleys refract the glitter
    and the garbage witch
    goes jumbling and peering
over the gutters' varied and various offerings
into cans that are sweet with the breath of July,
    the godless garbage of
    poor Mrs. Throstle
where the painful witch goes creaking and dying.

In the cell that rustles at night like a motion
the cell all complete and old with a nation
    that is always one,
    one only, one ever,
no star no sun no messenger moon
but insane time's face that shrinks and swells,
riven from God in her alter egos
    poor Mrs. Throstle
    poor Mrs. Throstle
her deity-decor all lewd and locked.

THE STARFISH

The great starfish was hauled up by a point.
Yellow and crimson with hard intricate bumps
it blazed wetly O it was regal and starry,
heavy cool cousin marine in the washy wave
a star a star.

But it was alive.

Its shape had a link with the steely stellar
steadfast light—no less than in ether
it conformed to its points of a star.

The sun strange as hot hell
attacked it in the grass. It could not
move. But it did. It
curled faintly

in the first sign of corruption—the distortion
of proportion,
of the correspondence between relative points. O a star
is not haphazard, only sickened
to death;
so, two points went
off center and the middle warped lightly.

It was a race.
Would the ants
clean it before irreparable corruption?
To gut a star
is a job—the ants were overtaxed.

There is a technique in destruction-through-preservation
                              of starfish:
To pleasure the pink lady's project a
gentle black boy
placed it on an anthill.

The ants worked, worked, small, shiny, quick.
They came too late; the
water's stellar space in the wave's wash
          or
the coral bed had corresponded to the nothing neighborhood
of a star.

Like a tide the light of color drew back, tide, tide
sucked by the wicked wick of sun:
the shape went even more off starshape.

The connection snapped.
Even before the ants finished
it had disappeared from the categories of desire

its silent cool marine starlife warm and warped
its starhood stung to chaos.

Here is your sting. O
death, where is your star?

SHADOW-POEMS

II. SHADOW-NOTE

There is this footnote to the shadow:
it has the cruelty of innocence.
It will neither make excuses nor give details,
As: this is how it happened . . .
Or: how worn his face was . . .

So that the particular body throws
the universal shadow on the sand,
carpet, pine-needles, cement, grave-sod,
telling one thing: the truth
without proportion, by its mass.

Where the substance would reach the doubtful senses
the shadow goes past, immediate and in depth,
to your most private recognition
of a gallows on gravel,
a cat on bright grass.

IV. SHADOW WATER-IMAGE

The houses waver in the water, waver,
flow over, stain and shudder.

Distorted, faithful, nothing is ignored,
all—contour, color—paired;

all—color, contour—changed. Untouchable:
water is brick and gable.

. . .

If the midnight heart, hunting love's face
meets in its place

his own, now will he drown, by such a loss,
in the silent brightness.

. . .

Narcissus, ravished, leaned a long moment
over this element:

the water-image then with a light shiver
drew down its lover

letting the fountain laughter play its gleam
over the rooted bloom.

PITCH LAKE

The underworld was beneath the earth's surface, but above the
nether waters, the great abyss.

Introduction to The Epic of Gilgamesh

Erishkigal, Ishtar's fresh sister, sky-
goddess, darkened to a queen of shadows,
she too a shade.
She never came back, unlike Persephone
released to gilded meadows
on the flowers' tide.

There are two motions here: Persephone's
and the sister's. The first led up
to the place known
and the face. The second, to where dust lies
on door and bolt, and hope drops.
That motion led down.

Through the Trinidad blaze no gaze can be trusted:
the pontooned truck seems motionless to our eyes
as we step warily where
like a desert but blueback, heaved, crested,
now, here, the pitch lake lies
in noon's stare.

Actually it is sinking—but so smooth, so light,
so noiseless . . . the men who shine and bake
to load it know;
one will leap to loose the pitch grip at the right
last instant—the stirred stiff lake
will let it go.

But its skeleton sister was caught in the bubble
of black, in the shift of shiny suck.
Someone was late.
So the men did their best by expensive trouble;
knowing the law of gravity-in-luck,
they gutted the wraith.

It is half under, gradually grim.
But only insects or the smallest mice
go where it goes,
except for minnows that appear and swim
in tiny pools like fissures in black ice
that open. And then close.

At all costs, no symbols—one motion
is up. The other, down. This bright
black sets forth
what is familiar to passion or caution.
Fatally knowing, we step, light-
ly, to fixed earth.

ARRIVAL OF RAIN

At midnight
it began to rain.

The sound of rain everywhere
fills my hollow ear.
The dry weeks round I was not thinking of that sound—
two sounds, the sound
of falling and the sound of drinking—
now here.

Dusty root darkens and the stubble sharpening
its cruel shafts, softens;
my hollow ear harkening
hears stubble green and moisten,
all drinking, all darkening;
the liquid beaded sigh
of sound, two sounds
everywhere and here
in the hollow avid ear.

All need is dry.
Rain is the metaphor.

FIEND, POET, IRIS

FOR MARY OWINGS MILLER

A passing fiend caught him changing from reader to writer.
First he was happy on a heath, or in a dark wood, was it?
Then jekyll-to-hyde, and the ardent successful reader
Gone. And what was there, the fiend knew exactly.

"You had something important to tell us?" the fiend
                                        said softly.
It watched him with amusement, stirring its wings.
He could only say, "I looked up, and something happened to
                                        that yellow iris."
"Something unique?" said the fiend, deadly sympathetic.

In its barbarous feathers, "Anon," said the fiend.
Rapidly it added, "Blake and Chaucer, Dante. And
                                        Euripides."
But before it found an F, he had said again,
Hopeless but helpless, "Something happened to the iris."

"Pride," said the fiend, casting up its eyebrows.
All its feathers shimmered. It raised a claw and said,
"Goethe; Hölderlin . . ." (here he lost track, thinking
Of the poems in Sanskrit, Greek and Persian)
                        ". . . Marlow," it was saying,

"Nerval, Ovid, Pushkin." (Pause.) "Quasimodo . . ."
He could see the iris suck its secret deeper,
"Racine," said the fiend from its snaky feathers,
"Shak—" here he flung a stone, which went through the fiend.

118

What had touched the iris, gone into, come out of,
Now he had no notion. All was still as shock.
Fiend went into feathers, feathers into fiend.
"Gentle fiend come back! Take the yellow iris!"

But no one knew—not Tasso, Ungaretti, Verlaine,
Not one knew what had happened to the iris;
He, on earth, in planets, galaxies, anywhere—
Only he, only he, only he must say.

VARIATIONS ON A THEME

Harlequin speaks by the moon's light:
By the light of the moon, Peter, my friend
Peter, from your dark window bend

(Dark and moon and shadow blend)
To listen at least. (The bare boughs soar,
Pencil the wild white snow) lend

Me your cold gold pen to write
By the bright moon, Peter, my friend,
One word. One single word, no more.

The cold step of the hungry whore
Strikes on the stone, the cold stars bend
Over my small dead candle-end,

My naked hearth is dead tonight
I have no fire there to mend.
For God's love, open your door.

FREIGHTER, FISH, MAN

The fish had leaped and leaped in the motion
of terror and down where the shadow of a shade
was lost it swam. There he sent word and emotion.
They foundered. When he raised his hand to shade
against the razzle-dazzle sea, the motion
cast on his wooden world a hand of shade.

In three bright leaps it had recomposed its sea.
It was alone: in that universe it would
meet nothing else nothing nothing. The sea
held not one other thing, nothing. The sea would
keep up and out his ship. He need not turn to see
behind him his masted world: vibration, words,
                                         and caulked wood.

In a cold wreck and wrack it spawned to swell
its trillion trillion, the salt sexual sea. That fish
was its only thing alive. In the long salt fertile swell
moved one alive. Felt itself swim, that fish,
mated with itself, ate itself. Swill and swell
deep débris sunstruck slant: "I" said that fish.

The spraysoaked beadbright teak of the rail of the ship
moved down and up, he rode his planks to stare
down through the glare glaze. "Worship," he said,
                                         "friendship."
Where the fish had gone with its silver and round stare
and universe of one, he tried to go; but the ship
stayed on top and the fish's sea refracted his stare.

In the blue, turquoise, black depth, in the glide dart and turn
that fish one cruised with downdrawn fishmouth saying "I"
forever and forever. Ship sails, sun shines, moon turns
all tides, but that ravenous mouth and unshuttered eye
goes alone round the sun round the moon round the sea, turns,
eternal turner, alone says only "I."

Some time away from the sea but still with salt
in his blood that keeps a tide, in the water
of his most bitter tears, some time away from the salt
swell that got him, he sees that fish under its tons of water
one thing in the ocean. Now he, feeling the spray's salt
on his skin, says "you" into the wind over the water.

49TH & 5TH, DECEMBER 13

I passed between the bell and the glass
window. Santa rang his bell. The wax girl leaned
forward: she was naked and had red nails.
Santa wore spectacles and rang his bell.
The second-floor trees raised rainbows in the dusk.

The snow fell lightly. I did not stop to ask
the scarlet man a favor; the girl leaned as if to give
from her wax body blood or heat or love.
But she was wax. Her belly and breasts were shaped;
she wore black pumps and leaned, above the pavement.

The unique snowflake died on the cement.
I passed between her wax eyes and his clapper.
The steelrimmed eyes watched me, the wax eyes watched
the watcher.
He rang, she leaned, to give me my message: that I must breed
alive unique love from her wax and his steel.

123

LANDSCAPE FINALLY WITH HUMAN FIGURE

The sky stainless, flawed by one gull
And stretched across no sight, silk-tight;
salt noon stranded like a hull
in clearest light;

clarity of palms splits the sun
to strike and shiver on the blue blue view,
so perfection not ended nor begun
is perfectly true.

The hollow setting (while the jewel lags),
infinite, unsoiled, smiling, clear:
      Appear!
Sly, dirty, cruel, lost and in rags
the beloved is here.

HOMAGE TO HENRI CHRISTOPHE

FOR LEON DAMAS

Vibrations of snow
pulse past the still boles:
the bare boughs move like a mobile of death.

In a Pennsylvania farmhouse I peer
through Quaker windows at the storm.
Ten thousand minutes ago I was in Haiti.

Cold cold cold. Toussaint in his Alpine cell,
dead, drawn up like a monkey from the cold
that froze the heat of Haiti in his blood.
Dying he spoke of Dessalines the Tiger, and of Henri
Christophe somewhere in the Haitian hills.

But they were too far away and it was too cold;
        and his fatigue must
have been enormous.

They were all tired, before the end, in one way or another;
Dessalines tired perhaps from hate
as the ash is the flame's fatigue. But then in pieces
                                in its bloody sack
his body rested.

Henri Christophe. L'Homme, they called him.
        Vive l'homme!
Grenada? St. Kitts? On some earth floor he
thrust   *his birth*
into the shock of breath.

That fortress against nothing. The Citadel. La Ferrière:
it rides its mountain, heavy with anger, rank
with pride; its great stone beak evil
prows into the evening green
like a ship. He mortared it with pain—
his own and others'.
He was a mason when he was a child.

II

The bats come out at dusk; at dusk
Haiti is always on the edge of something;
it stirs it stirs. The peaked stone shelter
built over the quicklime pit is still, however.

Liberty in his ear was foreign, in his blood
      native;   *his youth*
it ticked in his heart like a bomb.
A man's black young possession, he held
the horse and racked the billiard score.
That bony click on the green felt, he carried
to Sans Souci.
As a king, that is.

He saw so much while that bomb ticked like doomsday.
Ogé and Chavannes, at their torture.   *his youth*
A crowd followed the pitiful heads freed
from the body's wreckage.
Toussaint followed, and Dessalines. He watched,
and racked his score.

126

When he lay in his satin gown like a player,
with the silver bullet in the breach of his pistol—

his memories
on his deathbed

(he could hear the first snarl of the crowd,
the great palace—without care indeed—almost
empty, except that his daughters, named like players,
were in a room, Athénaire, Améthiste),
which were the ghosts?   *of the revolt*
Boukman and his bowl of blood hot from the boar
in Bois Caiman that night? the oath? blood
        vowed
in blood for blood?

Eight days eight nights, the circuses of blood
and the phoenix-breasted flame.
Dessalines, Toussaint. Christophe.
L'Homme. Vive l'homme!
He lifted the dark land. Fire, blood, sword, fire
but still the force was savage love
that knocked his blood in drumbeats in his ear,
to see the country shine, the green dark country.
He dragged it up the mountain on his back.

When did it change, that oldest serpent change?
The power in his blood turn to thick stone?
I saw a giant jungle mahogany, wound
in the arms of figuier maudit   *of his pride*
that sprang from a seed in a bird's feces:
thick as a devil, fluid in its hardness,
without a sound and over great time it killed.

Around his bones towers La Ferrière.

127

In the mad melodrama of dream   *of the priest's ghost*
this is familiar—the hot empty church
you burst into and knelt in extremity, and lifted
your eyes. There—his head still on his shoulders
          like a lie
moved the priest-celebrant.

It was the word you waited and you fell.   *of his stroke*
The jewel-goddess girls, the Duke of Lemonade,
the French priest's ghost, the palace and the   *of his haste*
          monstrous monument   *and his courage*
the silver bullet—true fairytales
to screen us from the black and dying man
who carried a land upon his back
while the bomb ticked too quickly for more
          than hope.

In sober fact, after the fairy bullet one man one woman
          and two girls
fought up the wicked path with that great
body. And this by dark.   *his burial in*
The new Haitian sun struck the inner court   *the limepit at*
like minted metal, and the quicklime,   *La Ferrière*
meant for bricks you understood,
sucked as it took you.
The dead citadel buries its dead.

But all that glory sank to green the forest
stain the great flowers and knit the roots.
There is a circle but it cannot hold you.
Liberty's lover breeds slavery from her flesh
and slavery breeds its parricide.
But the first day stays true.
Somewhere deep in the earth, dissolved in the sky like rain,
like rain, goes its own circle. You are free now.

The need for freedom is a desert-thirst.
You had it and you gave it.
This is a strange thing: ambushed by power like
    a fiend, yes, but
this was not the man.
His blood hums in the veins of rivers and
the red sun sheds it back on the rich earth.
Vive l'homme!

The Quaker storm shouts faster.
A mouse is at work
in the cold wall. The night gleams like a shell.

This thing is strange. You cannot spell
liberty. It is whole and avid for air.
Dark land in the blue sea, be free in him.

TREE ANGEL

Sang the angel in the tree:
pain prises the heart. See it stretch!
Narrow as the grave it was,
sang the leafy angel.

Fire in the marrow! sang
the angel in the tree,
pain pain on the inmost quick
another wave of it rises.

Pure pain taken
in the marrow the core the spirit's vein,
sang the birdly angel:
to your height it has added a cubit.

BALLAD OF THE FOUR SAINTS

Paul, that friend and heir to Christ,
Fought the tiger and the sea.
By the bloody ghost of Stephen
And the stones that let him free,
Paul—with Peter, Mary, Dismas—
Pray for us in charity.

The Magdelene while it was dark
Came to the tomb and found it empty.
By the violent common noon
Of your shame's discovery
Mary—with Paul, Dismas, Peter—
Pray for us in charity.

Peter, crucifixion's clown,
Died with earth where sky should be.
By your tongue of faithless friend
Quicker than the cockerel's cry,
Peter—with Dismas, Mary, Paul—
Pray for us in charity.

Dismas leapt to paradise,
Straight from wood to God went he.
By your clever thievish hand
Later struck upon the tree,
Dismas—with Mary, Paul and Peter—
Pray for us in charity.

Mighty saints who purify
Zealot, traitor, whore and thief,
Peter, Dismas, Mary, Paul,
Pray for us in charity.

PAINTER AT XYOCHTL*

He had a devil's look; and no rain—
The Mexican jungle rain-hungry,
The gods certainly angry,
The Mexican earth in dry pain—
The birds thirsty and the men and the grain.

But even with his mysterious coming, and his skin,
And the drought's brassy eye
The chief said, "Let him say.
If he is not a devil, let him begin—"
(Though he has come, and with the color of sin.)

In the dialect he could not say "Yes" or "No," "Old" or
                                                    "Young."
But the chiefs waited, even then,
While a runner fetched the men
(Two) who could speak the Outside tongue.
They were reasonable and patient, though the drought had
                                                    been long.

It was Spanish, of course. He could only plead
In English, in German. He cried, not in the Inside
Nor the Outside tongue, in his public need
He gibbered hell's speech.
But a devil can bleed.

Quartered, they carried him, within the rite,
North, South, East, West. The rains
Came promptly to the grains'
The men's, the birds' dry throats.
And flowers sprang like speech, to sight.

* A few years ago, a young German-American painter was the victim of
a ritual murder at the hands of some remote Central American Indians
into whose village he strayed alone during a prolonged drought.

THE GREEK WIND

This wind blows still in stone; blows
in still stone: this
stonestill wind lifts

the draped folds, rocks
the wing-tip, combs
back the stonecold curls.

The body breasts it, blown
almost back; the breasts are shaped
by the wind's touch: the breasts' breath

drinks it salt and fresh; in
the instant of centuries that salt
seawind bright

with invisibility, blows back
the fluent tender folds: watch
it tense the instep,

rush the neck's thrust. See:
it plows the stone like fluid wheat
in its passage.